# FINGERPRINTS, BITE MARKS, EAR PRINTS

# SOLVING CRIMES WITH SCIENCE:
# Forensics

# FINGERPRINTS, BITE MARKS, EAR PRINTS

Angela Libal

Mason Crest

Mason Crest
450 Parkway Drive, Suite D
Broomall, PA 19008
www.masoncrest.com

Printed and bound in the United States of America.

First printing
9 8 7 6 5 4 3 2 1

Series ISBN: 978-1-4222-2861-6
ISBN: 978-1-4222-2868-5
ebook ISBN: 978-1-4222-8954-9

The Library of Congress has cataloged the
hardcopy format(s) as follows:

Library of Congress Cataloging-in-Publication Data

Libal, Angela.
  Fingerprints, bite marks, ear prints / Angela Libal.
    p. cm. — (Solving crimes with science, forensics)
  Audience: 012.
  Audience: Grades 7 to 8.
  Includes bibliographical references and index.
  ISBN 978-1-4222-2868-5 (hardcover) — ISBN 978-1-4222-2861-6 (series) — ISBN 978-1-4222-8954-9 (ebook)
  1. Fingerprints—Juvenile literature. 2. Criminals—Identification—Juvenile literature. 3. Criminal investigation—Juvenile literature. 4. Forensic sciences—Juvenile literature. I. Title.
  HV6074.L532 2014
  363.25'8—dc23
                                            2013006940

Produced by Vestal Creative Services.   198 1202
www.vestalcreative.com

# Contents

# Introduction

*By Jay A. Siegel, Ph.D.*
*Director, Forensic and Investigative Sciences Program*
*Indiana University, Purdue University, Indianapolis*

It seems like every day the news brings forth another story about crime in the United States. Although the crime rate has been slowly decreasing over the past few years (due perhaps in part to the aging of the population), crime continues to be a very serious problem. Increasingly, the stories we read that involve crimes also mention the role that forensic science plays in solving serious crimes. Sensational crimes provide real examples of the power of forensic science. In recent years there has been an explosion of books, movies, and TV shows devoted to forensic science and crime investigation. The wondrously successful *CSI* TV shows have spawned a major increase in awareness of and interest in forensic science as a tool for solving crimes. *CSI* even has its own syndrome: the "*CSI* Effect," wherein jurors in real cases expect to hear testimony about science such as fingerprints, DNA, and blood spatter because they saw it on TV.

The unprecedented rise in the public's interest in forensic science has fueled demands by students and parents for more educational programs that teach the applications of science to crime. This started in colleges and universities but has filtered down to high schools and middle schools. Even elementary school students now learn how science is used in the criminal justice system. Most educators agree that this developing interest in forensic science is a good thing. It has provided an excellent opportunity to teach students science—and they have fun learning it! Forensic science is an ideal vehicle for teaching science for several reasons. It is truly multidisciplinary; practically every field of science has forensic applications. Successful forensic scientists must be good problem solvers and critical thinkers. These are critical skills that all students need to develop.

In all of this rush to implement forensic science courses in secondary schools throughout North America, the development of grade-appropriate resources that help guide students and teachers is seriously lacking. This new series: *Solving Crimes With Science: Forensics* is important and timely. Each book in the series contains a concise, age-appropriate discussion of one or more areas of forensic science.

Students are never too young to begin to learn the principles and applications of science. Forensic science provides an interesting and informative way to introduce scientific concepts in a way that grabs and holds the students' attention. *Solving Crimes With Science: Forensics* promises to be an important resource in teaching forensic science to students twelve to eighteen years old.

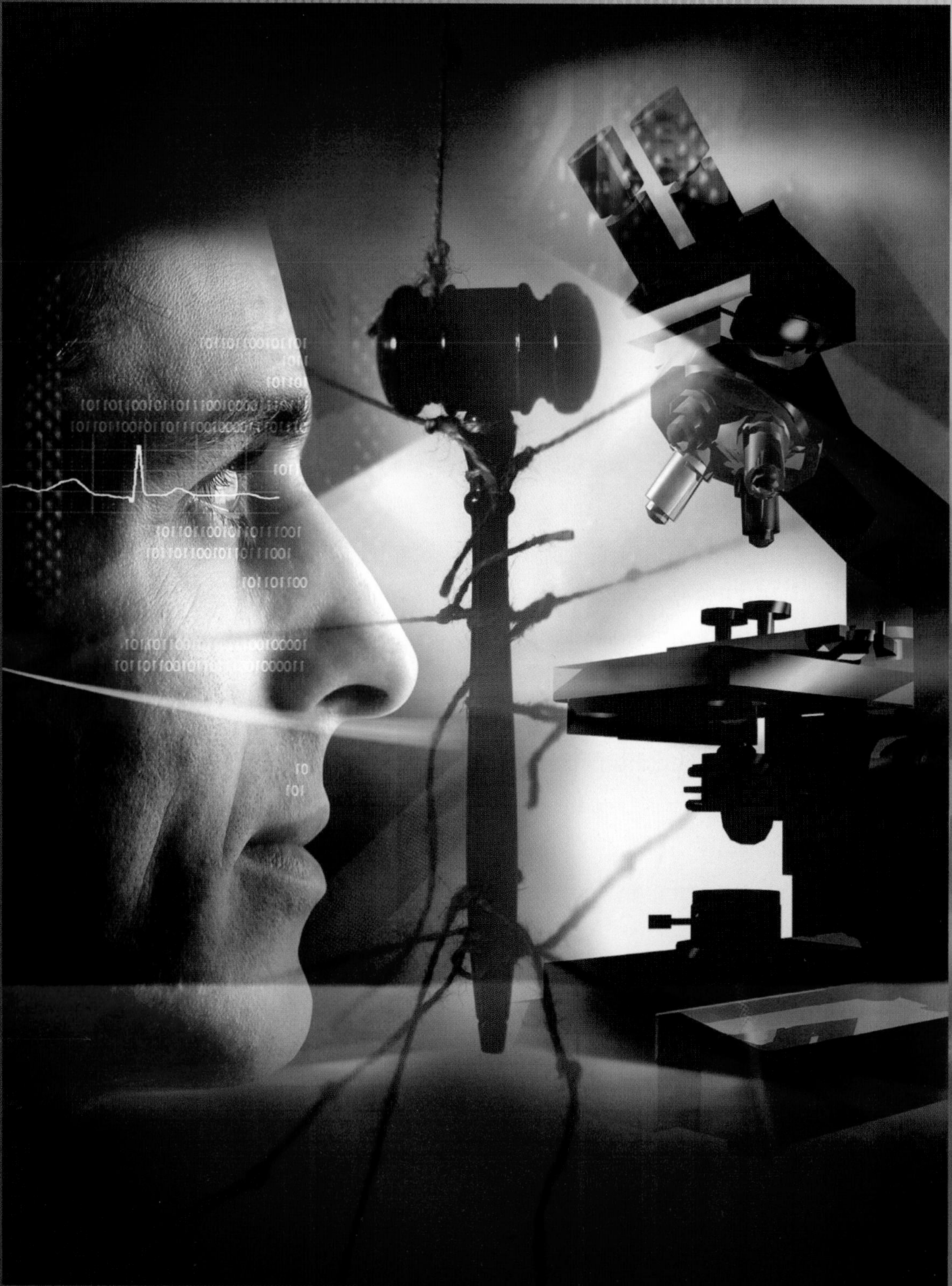

# Using Science in Criminal Investigation

In the early 1700s in Malta, Judge Cambo looked out his window one morning to investigate a commotion. He saw two men arguing. As one tried to run away, the other stabbed him in the back. The murderer, seeing Cambo watching, ran away, dropping his hat, knife, and sheath in his haste. Soon another man passed by and picked up the knife sheath before realizing he was at the scene of a murder. In his shock, he ran from the scene and was apprehended by police.

The unfortunate man eventually found himself before Judge Cambo, on trial for murder. Though Cambo had witnessed the entire crime, as a servant of the public law he decided he would be wrong to act on his personal knowledge. As was done in those times, the man was tortured in order to extract more information from him. Under torture, he confessed to the crime and was executed.

Many years later, another man, about to be executed himself, confessed to the murder. Judge Cambo's superior investigated Cambo's conduct; the fact that Cambo witnessed the crime and knew the man he had condemned was not the killer was brought to light. He was dismissed from his duties as judge, all the while protesting that he had behaved properly and impartially.

While the case of Judge Cambo is extreme, it is a good example of the need for a just and accurate way to identify criminals and clear the names of the innocent. The search for scientific methods of criminal investigation is a search for these types of human signposts.

# History of Criminal Investigation

North Americans have judicial systems based on codes of law. These codes require evidence, trials, and preponderances of evidence, or demonstration "beyond a reasonable doubt." In these systems, accused persons are innocent until proven guilty, judged by judges and juries based on the strength of evidence, and if found guilty, sentenced according to established rules for punishment. In our current systems, evidence must be presented, and proof of the accused's identity as the perpetrator is required. Scientific techniques are used to interpret many different kinds of evidence.

It was not always like this. Until the nineteenth century, science and the courtroom were strangers. The word "trial" means "a test," and tests of the accused were once very physical things. Through the European Renaissance, Middle Ages, and before, people could only be found guilty of crimes based on eyewitness testimony or confessions. Confessions, when not given freely, were procured by means of trial by ordeal—torture. This was true throughout most of the world.

Though scientific evidence is common in today's trials, that hasn't always been true. Trials by ordeal are described in the Bible.

Trials by ordeal are a very old practice. They are mentioned in some of our most ancient writings, including the Bible. The religious myths and texts of most cultures include some stories of trials by ordeal. In these trials, persons accused of crimes were subjected to some type of extreme act, such as carrying red-hot iron, drowning, or drinking poison. Gods or other supernatural beings were called on to intervene; it was thought that if a person were innocent, he would be protected by a supernatural being's

Throughout history, witch hunts fueled by lies and hysteria led to the deaths of innocent people. Public executions were meant to discourage others tempted to pursue witchcraft.

power. These trials were practiced well into the eighteenth century, including in North America, and were especially common in religious persecutions, such as the witch hunts carried on by the Catholic Church and later by some Protestant churches from the Middle Ages until the eighteenth century.

Related to trials by ordeal were trials by battle and vigilante justice. Trials by battle, such as duels, were direct confrontations between accused and accuser, usually with deadly weapons. The winner would be presumed right. Vigilante justice, or mob rule, was when people took the law into their own hands to punish people perceived as criminals. Done without courts or proof of guilt, vigilante justice led to the loss of many innocent

## Do Witches Float?

During the Inquisition, the Catholic Church's war on non-Christians and other misfits carried out during the Middle Ages and the Renaissance, some inquisitors developed a creative method of identifying "witches"—people accused of devil-worship or other non-Christian practices: they tied up the "witch" and threw her into a nearby body of deep water, such as a lake. If the "witch" floated, she was obviously being protected by evil magic, so she was taken from the lake, tortured, and executed. If the "witch" drowned, then she clearly had no magical powers and was innocent. Everyone could breathe a sigh of relief in these cases (except for the unfortunate lady, who was beyond breathing by that point) because the accused died a Christian and her soul was in heaven.

lives, such as in the lynchings of people of African descent in the United States between the Civil War and the middle of the twentieth century.

During earlier eras, when trials were carried out through the courts, evidence that identified individuals was not used. Rather, "justice" was based on eyewitness testimony and confessions. Eyewitness testimony usually required more than one witness; however, the fact that people sometimes lie was rarely taken into account. Testimony was considered a statement before God, and liars were said to be condemned to hell for all eternity. Courts did not take into consideration that the threat of eternal damnation might have little or no impact on some people. After an eyewitness testimony, the court required no further proof than a confession gained under torture.

In these earlier days in the world's history, torture was not only used by rogue **sadists** or in extreme circumstances: it was usually required by law. And once a person had confessed to a crime, there was no taking it back. No allowances were made for the fact that torture creates false confessions. The idea that a person would confess to a crime to end horrible suffering inflicted by her captors was, legally speaking, unthinkable. A person accused of a crime in those times usually had two options—death at the hands of her torturers in their attempt to wring a confession from her, or execution after confessing as punishment for the "crime."

Two factors of European society maintained the use of torture and kept the lack of evidence popular—religious control of states and a social class

Labor unions founded during the Industrial Revolution called for civil rights for all people. They helped develop the concept of equal justice for all used today.

structure of royalty and **serfdom**. The word of whichever church that controlled a nation was law and to disobey it was to be an enemy of the state and sentenced to execution. Also, society was divided into classes. Royals were believed to be born to power by the grace of God. Kings and queens made the law. If they themselves violated laws, there was almost nothing anyone could do about it. The structure of Europe was **feudal** for many centuries; royal families owned the land and everyone on it. Ordinary people were at the complete mercy of their rulers.

During the Enlightenment in European history, society began to change its thinking. Advances were made in science, churches began to lose some of their power, and separation of religion and state began. With **enclosure** of farmland and the **Industrial Revolution**, many common people were forced from their ancestral lands and into cities. The industrial workforce grew, and the old ways of looking at things changed. Eventually, workers began to organize into **labor unions** and to demand justice for ordinary people. All these things led to a broader demand for **civil rights** and justice under law.

With the founding of the United States, a nation was created without the rule of church or royalty. This had been unthinkable in the past, and its existence had a lasting effect on how law and justice would be pursued in the future throughout the world.

# The Rise of Evidence

Prior to the creation of modern courts and forensic science, the only evidence used in trials was circumstantial: evidence related to the circumstance of a crime, such as items from a crime scene found in a suspect's possession. Identifying evidence, like fingerprints, which identify a specific person, was unknown.

# Case Study:
# The Many Imaginary Crimes of Adolph Beck

One of the most famous cases of mistaken identity in all of criminal history is the case of Adolph Beck in Britain. One December day in 1895—before fingerprinting had come into vogue—he was stopped in the street by a woman who insisted he had stolen some of her jewelry. Certain that his innocence meant he had nothing to fear, Beck went with her to a police station, where officers listened to the woman's story. Unfortunately for Beck, several other women had recently told the same story about a man calling himself John Smith, and all the witnesses identified Beck as the thief. Based on their identifications and the testimony of a handwriting expert who judged that John Smith's handwriting matched Adolph Beck's, he was imprisoned and sentenced to seven years of hard labor.

In 1904, three years after his release on parole, another lady appeared in front of him in the street, loudly accusing him of stealing her jewelry. This time he ran . . . straight into the arms of a police officer. He was still in jail when John Smith, also known as William Thomas (real name Wilhelm Meyer) was finally arrested. Noting the striking similarity of their appearances, a detective took some of the women who had identified Beck to see Meyer, who they also identified immediately. Though fingerprinting had been in use since 1901, public outcry over the Beck case caused it to be adopted as the main criminal identification system in Britain.

Criminals can use many ways to disguise their identities. One thing that can't be changed is the eye, and retinal recognition is one high-tech method of identification.

When searching for a perpetrator, investigators would use a "needle in the haystack" approach. They would attempt to find a suspect's name or alias, and then track him, sometimes over hundreds of miles and many years. Imagine doing this in a world without telephones, computers, fingerprinting, photo identification, or even motor transport! Now consider that these limitations existed in a world without identification documents, where people could give false names or change their appearances at will, with no way to identify them except eyewitness accounts. Clearly, a systematic way to identify offenders was needed.

In 1882, Louis-Adolphe Bertillon developed the first system of physical identification. Initially tested by the police department he worked for in France, his method was so successful that within a few years, it had spread throughout Europe and the European colonies of the world. Bertillon's method was called anthropometry, or bertillonage. It involved taking exact measurements of eleven different parts of a person's body and filing the identification reports according to these measurements for future reference. Based on the idea that no two human beings are exactly alike, anthropometry was hugely successful at identifying repeat criminal offenders. Also, it planted the idea that human beings can be accurately identified by

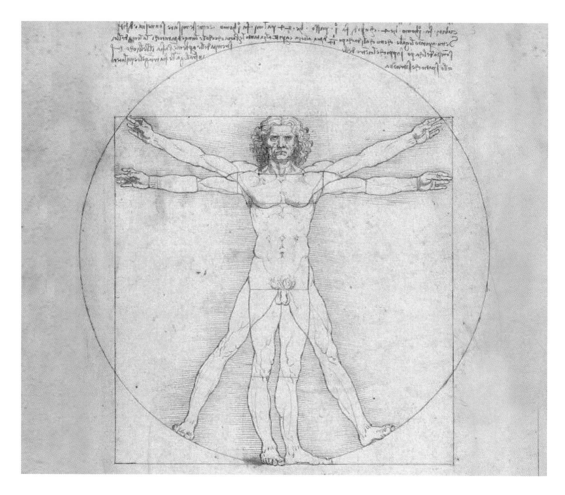

Louis-Adolphe Bertillon thought that human beings could be positively identified through the measurements of specific body parts.

unique individual characteristics, which is what our criminal identification system is based on today.

# Classification of Evidence

There are two classifications of evidence: evidence with class characteristics only (or circumstantial evidence), and evidence with individual identifying characteristics.

Class character evidence can have more than one source. Soil, weapons, anything that could have been left at the crime scene by more than one individual falls under this classification.

Individual identifying character evidence can only be left by one person. Fingerprints, bite marks, handwriting—these are unique and require the presence of one particular person at the crime scene.

Some types of evidence can fit in either category, depending on their context. Blood or hair can yield DNA, which is identifying, but also could have been brought onto a crime scene in more than one way, which would make it circumstantial. For example, hair found at a crime scene could have been shed there by the perpetrator, or it could have been left by an innocent prior visitor to the location, been brought in on someone's clothing, or been planted by a perpetrator attempting to frame someone else. Shoeprints, toolmarks, paint chips, anything that could have come from more than one place is circumstantial until it can be definitively proven to match a specific item in the possession of a specific person. (Microscopic analysis can sometimes do this by matching marks and patterns that are impossible to see with the naked eye.)

# Interdisciplinary Nature of Forensics

The science of criminal investigation has advanced tremendously since the days of trials by ordeal and court-mandated torture. Today many investigatory scientific techniques use a wide variety of scientific fields that overlap and work together. This is called an interdisciplinary, or multidisciplinary, approach. While we can talk about just one area, such as fingerprinting, all areas of the forensic sciences—forensic anthropology, *entomology*, psychology, document analysis, fiber analysis, *serology*, DNA analysis, *ballistics* analysis, and others—must work together to successfully solve crimes, bring criminals to justice, and *absolve* the innocent.

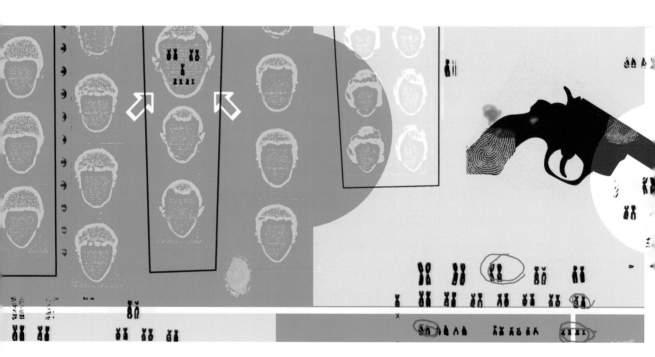

Scientific evidence can play an important role in the justice system. Blood found on weapons and at the scene can rule out suspects, for example.

Even the smallest piece of evidence could be important in solving a crime. Investigators look for the unexpected and the out-of-place at a crime scene.

Mishandling of evidence, failure to collect or record all evidence, inappropriate behavior on the part of law enforcement professionals, and placing ego or other personal issues over the search for the truth is just as damaging as having no evidence at all. In some cases, it can be even worse than a lack of evidence, as mishandling of evidence and the use of improper legal procedures have the power to send innocent people to prison or death. Law enforcement personnel have chosen a profession with tremendous responsibility. They literally hold the lives and freedom of others in their hands. The impartial search for the truth must always be their top priority.

**Using Science in Criminal Investigation**

No matter how conclusive evidence might be, if not collected properly, it may be inadmissible at trial. Care must be taken not to contaminate evidence.

# How Is Evidence Used in Criminal Trials?

Laws strictly govern the collection of evidence and its use in criminal trials. These laws state when it's appropriate to gather evidence, procedures for gathering evidence, how this evidence is to be protected and stored, who is allowed access to it, and how it may be presented to jurors and judges during a trial.

Laws of search and seizure and due process state when and how law enforcement officials are allowed to enter locations and claim property as evidence. Abiding by these rules is the first step in evidence gathering. If these laws are not followed, even the most incriminating evidence will not be admissible during a trial.

A crime scene must be thoroughly investigated to uncover all the clues.

Human signpost evidence, along with all biological samples such as blood and other sources of DNA, are scientific specimens that must be collected and recorded in proper ways. Technicians who collect these pieces of evidence must be carefully trained, and many jurisdictions also require they be certified by a local government authority.

Once a piece of evidence is collected, a chain of custody is established that must not be broken. This means that it is kept within the custody-of-evidence handlers who record where it is and who has access to it at all times. If the chain of custody is broken, the evidence will no longer be admissible in a trial.

At trial, forensic scientists must present evidence so that jury members can understand. This can be difficult when the information is "dry" and technical.

After collection, experts in the field must review the evidence. Finger-prints are useless without someone who knows how to examine them and how to search for a match. This is true for all types of physical evidence. Its usefulness is only as good as the competence of investigators and expert witnesses.

Finally, when the evidence has been collected, analyzed, and has a properly documented chain of custody, the court—judges, prosecutors, and defense attorneys—will decide which pieces of evidence will be admitted for consideration during a trial.

# Ethics and Law Enforcement

The role of judges and juries is to review all the evidence and, in accordance with the law, come to a decision based on that evidence. Forensic investigators must never think of themselves as part of the prosecutorial team (or, for that matter, of the defense). The judicial system requires they be impartial and objective, and only offer the facts without embellishing them with any personal opinion that is not scientifically based. If an investigator ever allows presentation of the evidence to be influenced by personal bias, it can lead to grave miscarriages of justice that could deprive innocent people of their freedom or even their lives, while allowing true criminals to escape punishment.

The history of forensic investigation is a history of moving closer to this goal. The discoveries of individual identifying evidence and scientific techniques of processing this evidence are signposts on this path.

# 2

# By These Signs Ye Shall Know Him: Fingerprints

Scientific crime investigation and human identification are based on two principles, scientific theories that are supported by so much evidence that they must be accepted as fact. The first is Locard's Principle: every contact leaves a trace. No matter where someone goes or what someone does, there is always evidence left behind. Clothing fibers, dust, hairs, fingerprints: there is always an exchange of some material in any contact. This principle is why the forensic sciences are possible. The second is the Principle of Individuality: each human being is unique, which is why fingerprints and other imprints can be used to identify people precisely.

Fingerprints were first used for identification in the ancient Roman and Chinese empires, where they were occasionally used to sign contracts, works of art, and criminal confessions. It is also said that a palm print was used to solve a crime in Rome as far back as the first century CE. However, prints' real potential in criminal investigation was not realized until the nineteenth century.

## The First Fingerprint Case

The first time fingerprints were used to solve a criminal case was in Argentina in July of 1892, after Francisca Rojas' two children were found bludgeoned to death in their beds. Rojas accused a neighbor, whom she claimed to have seen fleeing her house.

Fingerprints have been used in criminal identification since the late nineteenth century.

## Case Study: Edmund Locard

Locard was a French police investigator who lived from 1877 until 1966. A big fan of the famous fictional detective Sherlock Holmes (a creation of the writer Sir Arthur Conan Doyle), Locard applied Holmes's techniques and the techniques of Hans Gross, who is known as the first forensic scientist. Locard originally called his principle "the problem of dust." He used this "problem" to solve many cases despite the skepticism of his superiors. Cases he solved include a strangulation, where he found the victim's face powder underneath the fingernails of the murderer, and coin counterfeiting, where he found microscopic metal dust on the counterfeiters' clothing.

The neighbor was taken into custody, but he refused to admit to the crime. Determined to gain a confession, the police chief tortured him for two weeks; the process included tying him up and forcing him to spend the night on a bed with the corpses of the two children. When the man still refused to confess, the chief of police began to search for other suspects. He returned to the crime scene to look for clues while Francisca Rojas was away at work, and found a bloody fingerprint on the doorframe. The wood with the print was removed and brought to the police station, and Rojas was fingerprinted. The prints were compared. The one on the doorframe came from her right thumb.

Remembering that Rojas claimed she had not touched the children's bodies, the police chief questioned her and showed her the evidence. She

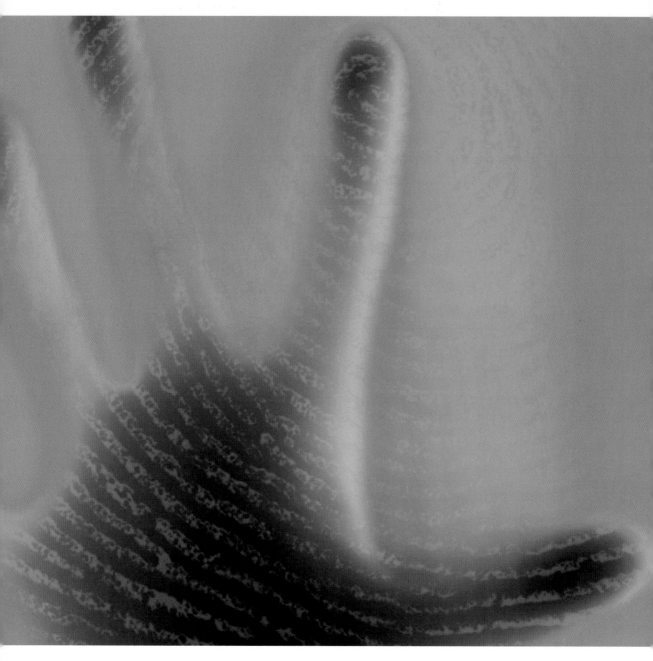

Because everyone's fingerprints are unique, these prints can be used to identify bodies and suspects. The loops and whirls have put many criminals in prison.

FINGERPRINTS, BITE MARKS, EAR PRINTS

admitted to the murder of her own children, hoping that her new boyfriend would marry her if only she were childless.

# The Discovery of Fingerprints

European scientists had begun to write about finger-, hand-, and footprints in the 1600s, but little came of it at the time. Czech physiologist and biologist Joannes Evangelista Purkinje discovered that each person's fingerprints are unique in 1823, but this theory was not yet tested, and fingerprints were not used for identification. In 1858, William Herschel, who was working for the British Empire in India, began asking people to sign contracts and receipts with hand- or fingerprints to end cheating. Nearly twenty years later, he suggested that this method could be used in criminal identification.

While Herschel was working in India, a doctor and **physiology** professor named Henry Faulds was working with fingerprints in Tokyo. Faulds had noticed the distinctive marks left in Japanese pottery by the potters' fingerprints, and studied these marks and the **papillary lines** on human fingertips. Also realizing that each person has a unique set of prints, he assisted in solving several burglary cases and clearing innocent suspects.

Both Faulds and Herschel wrote letters about their discoveries to the scientific magazine *Nature*. While Faulds felt that Herschel was trying to "steal" the fame for his discovery, they are both considered the fathers of modern fingerprinting. By 1906, fingerprinting had become the basic method of identification in criminal investigations around the world.

# 3

# Let Your Fingers Do the Talking

Fingerprints, palm prints, and footprints are caused by the whorls and ridges of human skin on these areas of the body. Several months before birth, these ridges form, extending all the way through the skin's many layers. In fact, even if the skin over the fingertips is removed, the prints will grow back in exactly the same pattern as the fingertips heal.

## Latent Fingerprints

Human skin contains sebaceous (oil) glands and sweat glands. These glands are constantly secreting fluid to the skin's surface, even when we don't feel sweaty or oily. Every touch by skin leaves some of this residue behind—and this is what creates latent prints. Latent prints are prints that cannot be seen with the eyes alone. They must first be developed.

# Case Study:
# The Most Famous Bank Robber In History

From May of 1933 to July of 1934, John Dillinger committed a string of bank robberies across the United States. He was so successful at robbing banks and avoiding the authorities that then-director of the FBI, J. Edgar Hoover, declared him "Public Enemy Number One." Dillinger's hunted lifestyle took its toll in stress, however, and he tried to find a way to blend back into peaceful society.

He decided to change his face with plastic surgery, and to have his fingerprints removed. His first fingerprint-ectomy, which involved slicing the skin from his fingers, was unsuccessful, and nearly killed Dillinger when he swallowed his tongue while under anesthesia. The second operation involved burning the prints off with acid. Dillinger could have saved himself the pain and trouble. A few months later he was betrayed by an ex-girlfriend and shot by Hoover's agents outside a movie theater . . . and his fingerprints had already reappeared.

The method used to develop prints depends on the type of surface on which they were left. When investigators suspect that a surface may have fingerprints, they choose a development method. While there are over forty different techniques used to develop prints, they fall into three basic categories: dusting for nonporous surfaces, fuming for semiporous surfaces, and chemical development for porous surfaces.

Though often criticized, J. Edgar Hoover helped build the FBI into a crime-fighting giant. Unfortunately, he also used the organization to spy on innocent citizens.

Nonporous surfaces are completely nonabsorbent, and include glass, porcelain, ceramic, polished metal, or sealed (painted or varnished) wood. Latent prints are developed on these surfaces by dusting the surface with a gray (for dark surfaces and highly reflective surfaces such as mirrors or chrome) or black (for light-colored surfaces) powder. This powder sticks to the oil and perspiration, showing an impression of the print. The print is

**Let Your Fingers Do the Talking** **35**

first photographed with a special fingerprint camera, then lifted with tape. This tape can be transparent or opaque, but its color must contrast with the color of the powder. The tape is transferred to a card whose color also contrasts with the color of the print.

Semiporous surfaces are somewhat absorbent, like brick, rocks, some metal objects (including guns), some wood, plastic, rubber, vinyl, leather, and the bodies of victims. The process used to develop prints on these surfaces is called fuming. In fuming, the investigator heats a wand made of a substance called cyanoacrylate (commonly known outside of forensics as Super Glue). The wand is waved near the surface, and the vapor from the cyanoacrylate adheres to the prints. Smaller objects may be placed in a fuming cabinet where they are exposed to the substance with or without heat. The prints are then photographed. The entire fumed object becomes evidence because the prints cannot be lifted. They must be studied directly on the object or from the photographs.

Porous surfaces are completely absorbent. Paper and untreated wood are examples of such surfaces. Prints on these types of surfaces are developed using the chemical method. A substance made of the chemicals iodine, ninhydrin, and silver nitrate is spread over the surface. This makes any prints become dark, and they are then photographed. This type of developed print can also be lifted.

Prints can also be collected using an electrostatic procedure. This is especially useful if the prints are very delicate or faint, or on colored surfaces. The prints are dusted, then covered with lifting film. A power source sends an electric charge through this film that attracts the dust. The transferred prints are then photographed.

Investigators can sometimes check surfaces for latent prints before dusting, fuming, or chemically treating items. This is done with laser beams or a high-intensity, specially filtered light called an Alternate Light Source

(ALS). When viewed in a dark room, these types of light make the substances in the prints *fluoresce*. This method can also be used for other bodily excretions, including blood and urine. Some new chemical methods are also being developed that, when sprayed on, can reveal fingerprints on human skin.

# Case Study: The Mysterious Printless Fingers of Robert Phillips

Around the same time John Dillinger was robbing banks, Robert Phillips was making a career as a successful hold-up man, until he was caught stealing a car and jailed for ten years. After his release, he resumed his former profession but was eager to erase his record and avoid another jail term. A doctor named Leopold Brandenburg came up with an ingenious plan—graft skin from another part of his body onto his fingertips. Phillips' fingerprint skin was removed. He then sat for three weeks with his fingers strapped to open wounds on his chest, waiting for the skin to grow over them. Unlike Dillinger's surgery, Phillips' operation was successful—but he, too, could have saved himself the time, money, and pain. When he was arrested again, police were so suspicious of his lack of fingerprints that they tossed him into jail until they could find a crime with which to match him. Eventually, a small print from his lower-left ring finger was matched to a print from the same area that had accidentally been inked during a prior arrest.

# Patent and Plastic Prints

Two types of fingerprints are not caused by the skin's own oils: patent prints and plastic prints. Patent prints are left by a foreign substance on the fingers, such as grease, blood, or paint, and are visible to the unaided eye. Plastic prints are prints that are left in a substance like mud or food.

Patent prints and plastic prints, as well as any type of print left on greasy or wet surfaces, should not be developed. The procedure instead is to photograph these types of prints. Plastic prints—those that leave an

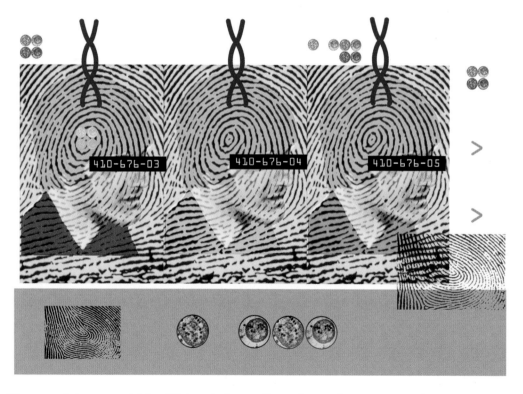

410-676-03    410-676-04    410-676-05

Fingerprints reveal identifying information about the person who committed a crime. Careful analysis can point the finger at the perpetrator and eliminate other suspects.

indented impression in a substance or object—can also sometimes be cast with an alginate or plaster mold. This mold can then be studied.

Patent prints left with blood or other body fluids can be especially useful due to the multidisciplinary nature of forensic work because body fluids leave behind chemical traces, even after a surface looks clean. Special lights can be used to make these traces fluoresce, or chemical methods can be used to develop these body fluid stains. These chemical methods are similar to the fuming and chemical methods used for fingerprint development.

One of the most common and effective chemical methods uses hydrogen peroxide and a substance called ortho-tolidine. When the ortho-tolidine comes into contact with hydrogen peroxide in the presence of blood residue, a certain molecule in red blood cells makes the chemical turn blue. Using this method, investigators can see prints that would have been incomplete or invisible to the eyes alone.

# Classification of Prints

Fingerprints are classified by the shapes of the skin's papillary ridges. There are four main types: arches, loops, whorls, and accidentals or composites (although some researchers consider these to be a subtype of whorls). They are subdivided into more categories, with arches being either plain or tented; loops radial or ulnar; and whorls as plain, central pocket loops, or double loops. Each person usually has more than one type of fingerprint, since a different type can be on each finger.

When prints are compared, they are examined by experts. If they look like a close match, the fingerprint experts look for exact points of comparison and mark them. The number of exact points of comparison that need to be marked for the fingerprints to be used as identifying evidence depends

# Case Study: Ghostly Prints

Many techniques have been created to fingerprint dead bodies. But fingerprinting a ghost? An attempt to do exactly that was made in England in 1961 by Sergeant Rowland Mason of the Fingerprint Bureau of the Greater Manchester Police. He was asked to do this by a researcher of the paranormal who had been investigating the case of a violin-playing ghost named Nicholas for two years. The ghost apparently resided in a small house with a woman and her young son and daughter. He had begun to make himself known when the boy started taking violin lessons, and was reportedly heard at night in the boy's room, playing the violin with amazing skill. The boy's mother approached Manchester's Society for Psychical Research, which held séances attempting to contact Nicholas. Reportedly, a pair of ghostly hands could be seen at these séances, and the paranormal investigator wanted to have them fingerprinted to compare them to the prints of everyone in the room to expose a hoax. After watching objects, including a tambourine, mysteriously move during a séance, Mason decided he would like to give it a try.

At the next séance, Mason held the ghostly hands. Thus convinced, he polished the tambourine, hoping to use it to capture ghostly prints. It flew around the room at the next séance, but when he dusted it for prints, he could find none. Again he attended a séance, this time dusting the tambourine with fingerprint powder first. Again, no marks. Finally the investigators asked Nicholas if they could take his prints. Mason took one of the ghostly hands and pushed it into the ink and then onto the fingerprint pad . . . but when the pad was examined later, all that could be found were three scratches.

Giving up on further fingerprinting attempts, the investigators asked Nicholas if he would allow them to photograph him. He was asked to sit in an armchair, and a photograph was taken with infra-red light. The picture showed the armchair with a crease on the head cushion, behind the faint image of a very old, bearded man. The Detective Chief Inspector of the Fingerprint Bureau, Tony Fletcher, later wrote, "If you were now to ask me if I believe in ghosts, I would reply that I do not readily disbelieve."

on the laws of the area. On average, about fifteen points of comparison must be demonstrated. If only a certain number of matching points are marked, it does not mean that other points do not match. It simply means that this is the number needed to demonstrate to nonexperts that the prints match. Today, computers are used to make these detailed comparisons.

# Fingerprinting Suspects

Suspects are fingerprinted by pressing each fingertip firmly onto a pad of ink, then onto a fingerprint card with a separate box for each finger. The fingertip is pressed onto the pad and gently rolled once from left to right. The fingerprint card is then filed and cross-referenced according to the type of prints.

Computer and laser technology have begun to be used to take inkless fingerprints. Fingertips are placed over a scanner that reads the prints and copies them onto a computer file.

# Fingerprints of Missing Persons and Unidentified Decedents

It can be very difficult to identify bodies based on fingerprints. Unless a person has fingerprints on file in a criminal or missing-persons database, or unless her identity is suspected, there will be nothing with which to

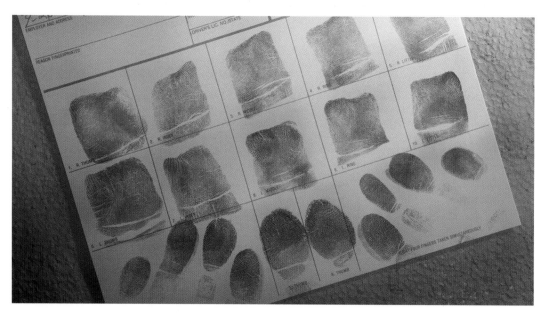

Investigators once spent long hours—even days or weeks—going through fingerprint cards to find a match. Today, computer-scanned fingerprints make the search much faster.

compare the fingerprints. A person who has been arrested will have fingerprints on file with law enforcement agencies, so this is the first place where investigators look for a match. If no match is found here, there are still other options.

If a possible identity has been found for an unidentified body, investigators can look for his prints in a few places. Some jobs require fingerprinting, for example, particularly government jobs or jobs requiring licenses. Also, various attempts have been made to keep files of schoolchildren's fingerprints so there will be matches in missing persons' cases. Latent prints can also be taken from the homes or belongings of people who have gone missing, in the hope of matching them to unidentified persons.

When a body is found before the hands have reached a stage of advanced decomposition, the body is fingerprinted by inking the fingertips

Fingerprints are also used to identify victims. Many children have been fingerprinted in case they are lost—or kidnapped.

# Case Study:
# Dangerous Women

Between 1989 and 1990, the bodies and abandoned cars of seven middle-aged men were discovered along Florida highways. The first corpse was found in a state of advanced decomposition. His hands were removed and sent to a crime lab for fingerprinting. They had to be soaked in saline solution for several hours until the skin was tight and strong enough for prints to be taken. They were matched to a man who had once been arrested for drunk driving. This man was also the owner of a car abandoned several days earlier. That car, and each found after it, had been wiped clean. No fingerprints could be located, but there were witnesses.

Two women had been seen leaving the car of one of the victims. Forensic artists made sketches based on the descriptions. Several people contacted police claiming to recognize the suspects. Meanwhile, police began searching for items that could have been stolen from the murdered men. They hit a stroke of good luck. In a pawnshop, an investigator found two items stolen from the car of one of the victims. According to Florida law, the pawner had placed her thumbprint on the pawnshop receipt.

Investigators used this thumbprint and the names given to them by people who had seen the sketches to trace the two women. They soon matched the print to a woman with many aliases and a long and violent criminal record. Meanwhile, a bloody handprint turned up in one of the victim's cars. This matched the thumbprint on the receipt. Within days, Aileen Wuornos was arrested. Her partner agreed to cooperate with police in exchange for not being charged with the crimes, which she claimed she did not commit. Wuornos soon confessed to the seven murders, making her the most famous female serial killer in North America.

and wrapping the fingerprint cards around them. However, if the person has been deceased for a length of time, this gets trickier.

If a body is decomposing and fingerprints can no longer be seen with the ink-pad method, there are several options. Sometimes investigators will inject a mixture of glycerin and water underneath the skin to round the fingertips so they have the shape of living fingers, which can then be inked and printed. The skin may also be cut from the hand and flattened for printing. If fingerprints can no longer be taken traditionally because of advanced decomposition, they can sometimes still be taken with laser scanning. Another method is to dust the tips of the fingers with various compounds and then photograph or x-ray them.

At a certain state of decomposition, a body's skin sloughs off and often can be found in dried pieces near the body. These particles of skin can sometimes be rehydrated and the prints taken from them.

When a body is found in water, the skin is often only loosely connected to the body. A process called degloving is used to fingerprint these bodies. This means that an investigator cuts the skin and carefully rolls it off the hands of the corpse. She then rolls the skin over her own hand, which she first covers with a latex glove, and then fingerprints herself with the corpse's skin.

If a body is dried or mummified, the hands must be soaked in chemicals to soften the flesh and make it pliable enough to show prints. The hands are then fingerprinted, or the skin is removed and the degloving method is used.

If local investigators are unable to do the printing, the hands are removed, placed in a preservative solution, and mailed or transported to a laboratory that has the necessary equipment. Often several of these methods are used in a single investigation.

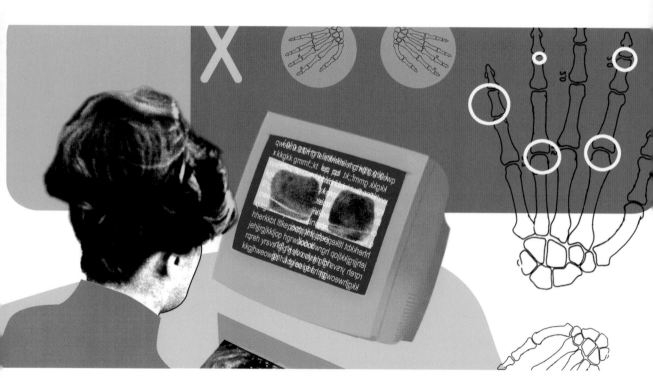

Fingerprint databanks make it harder for criminals to avoid pursuit. Law enforcement agencies can access databanks worldwide to identify criminals.

# Canada's Real Time Identification Project

Canada has an extensive database of fingerprints on file, accessible to the Royal Canadian Mounted Police (RCMP). In the past, fingerprint databases relied on paper processes. Law enforcement officials want access to fingerprints to be even easier, and have been working to update the databases by making them electronic. Fingerprint records are now part of the Canadian Criminal Real Time Identification Services (CCRTIS), allowing access from stations all over the country. Law enforcement can now identify criminals and victims faster and easier.

# Fingerprint Databanks

Collecting fingerprints is only helpful if there are known fingerprints with which to make comparisons. This is why government agencies maintain computerized databanks of fingerprint cards so that crime-scene prints and the prints of unidentified suspects and decedents can be compared against the databases.

The largest fingerprint database in the United States is called the IAFIS, the Integrated Automated Fingerprint Identification System. The IAFIS is maintained by the federal government and contains fingerprint records of everyone who has ever been arrested in the United States, foreign nationals who have been detained by immigration officials, and prints collected at

# Case Study:
# The Two Will Wests

The case of the two Will Wests occurred in 1903 when a new prisoner appeared at Leavenworth penitentiary for processing. At the time, the prison used bertillonage to identify its inmates. The clerk announced that he had seen Will West before and that his measurements were already on file. West denied having ever been in Leavenworth. Growing angry, the clerk searched the records and, sure enough, retrieved Will West's photograph and measurements. West continued to deny that he had ever been in the prison. Losing his temper, the clerk finally asked prison guards about Will West, only to discover that he was already imprisoned at Leavenworth. Their bertillonage measurements were compared and were only slightly different, but their fingerprints were extremely different. This case cemented the use of fingerprints to identify prisoners in the United States.

The story was not yet over, however. While the tale of the two identical Will Wests seemed amazing at the time, some modern investigators insist that it is not all that it appears. They claim that, while in Leavenworth together, the two Will Wests wrote letters to the same mother, the same brothers and sisters, and the same aunt. The Wests are now thought to have been brothers, possibly identical twin brothers, Will and Bill West.

crime scenes. The U.S. IAFIS estimates that it received over 61 million sets of prints in 2010 alone.

The FBI maintains the IAFIS and oversees around twenty-four fingerprint databases. The other databases that are used most often are the NCIC, and the NICBCS. The NCIC is the National Crime Information Center. It keeps fingerprint records of missing persons, fugitives, people on probation and parole, convicted sex offenders, and fingerprints connected to vehicle thefts. It estimates that it receives about 7.9 million requests for information per day. The NICBCS is the National Instant Criminal Background Check System—the system that checks the criminal-record histories of gun buyers in the United States.

Investigators can lift fingerprints from a keyboard used by a suspect.

The United States also maintains IDENT, the Automated Biometric Identification System, through its Homeland Security Department. There is an ongoing debate about which government agencies should have access to this system.

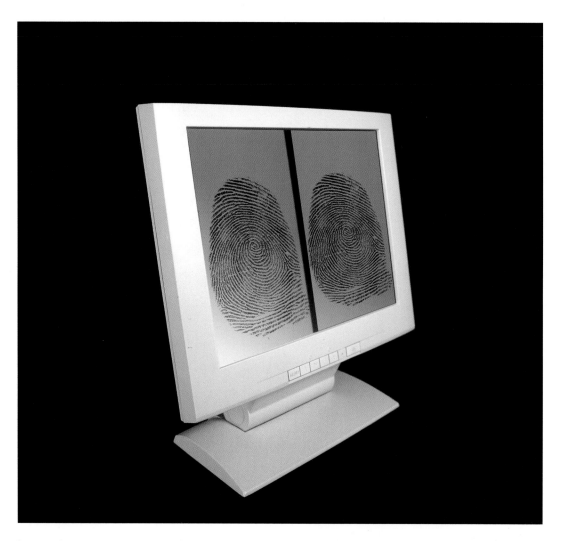

Investigators must carefully analyze a fingerprint's characteristics. They can use fingerprints on file in their system, and in the systems of other agencies, to determine a match.

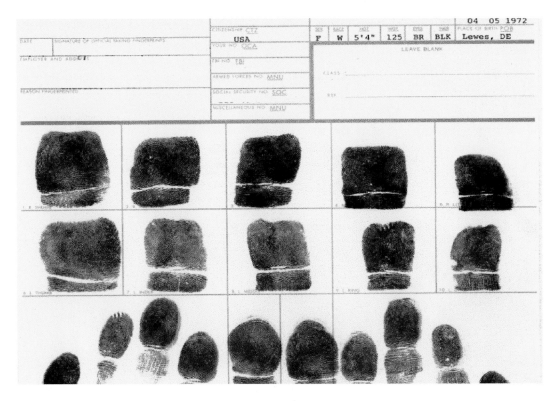

Job applicants may be fingerprinted for their employer's records.

In addition to these databases, the United States has several thousand local law enforcement databases with fingerprint records. A major complaint in trying to match prints is that the right database may not always be searched. This can be a serious problem, since local databases are not linked to each other. In addition, many state computer systems are not linked to the FBI, and some of the FBI's systems are not even linked to each other.

This lack of communication can severely affect criminal investigations, as was seen in the 2002 sniper shooting case of John Allen Muhammad and John Lee Malvo. Operating in Alabama, Virginia, and Washington,

Many criminals wear gloves to avoid leaving fingerprints—but they often don't wear them when loading a gun, which means they leave behind prints on the bullets.

Fingerprints left by Washington, D.C.-area snipers in 2002 helped to identify the shooters. Miscommunication between law enforcement agencies, however, delayed the identification.

D.C., Muhammad and Malvo eluded officers during a month-long shooting spree, killing ten people and terrorizing communities.

After the first shooting, investigators in Alabama collected fingerprints left by Malvo. These prints remained unidentified for twenty-three days because Alabama's state law enforcement computer system is not linked to the FBI's, so the FBI's fingerprint databases were not searched. When the hunt for the snipers became a federal investigation, FBI inspectors compared the fingerprints to their databases and found a match within two hours.

# Bite Marks

Bite marks have occasionally appeared as evidence in criminal trials throughout history. It was not until the 1970s, though, that they became commonly introduced as evidence in North American courtrooms.

Possibly the most famous trial to ever rely on bite-mark evidence occurred in Florida. On January 15, 1978, a University of Florida sorority house was broken into, and two young women were later found beaten and strangled. Three others had also been violently attacked.

The police eventually arrested Ted Bundy, a former law student who had crossed paths with police in the past. He was considered a suspect in a string of brutal murders of young women and girls across at least four states. The killings were thought to have begun in Washington State in 1969, with the abduction and murder of a fifteen-year-old girl who was running away from home. After abducting, torturing, raping, and brutally murdering several women in the area, he moved to Utah, then to Colorado, continuing his killing spree, and eventually ending up in Florida. After attacking the five college students, he kidnapped and murdered a twelve-year-old girl before being stopped by police for a traffic violation and arrested.

No fingerprints had been found at the crime scenes. It was his bite marks in the flesh of one of the sorority-house victims that finally brought him to justice. They were unusually clear and showed a unique pattern of the perpetrator's bottom teeth, with the canines overlapping the incisors.

After his arrest, Bundy at first refused to submit to an oral examination, until the court forced him to have photographs and casts made of his teeth. These were compared to the victim's wounds and were clearly a positive match. After his conviction, Bundy told the story of his murders of at least twenty-four young women. He was executed in the electric chair in Florida in 1989.

# Human Dentition

Like all other forms of evidence, bite marks have both class and individual characteristics. Class characteristics are what define the bite mark as human. This includes the size and shape of the jaws, and the dentition, which is the number and type of teeth. Human beings, like each type of animal, have a distinct dentition. Adult human dentition is three-two-one-two, which means three molars, two premolars, one canine tooth, and two incisors on each side of each jaw. After determining that the bite mark came from a human, experts can examine the mark and decide if it came from an adult or a child, and which parts were made by the mandibular arch (the lower jaw), and which by the maxillary arch (the upper jaw).

After studying these class characteristics, investigators look for individual characteristics that may identify a perpetrator. These characteristics will help match the bite marks to the biter.

According to criminologists, bite marks are most common in sex murders and in the murders of battered children by caregivers. Bite marks in sexually motivated murders are usually found on the breasts and lower body, while bite marks on abused children are often found all over the body. Criminal psychologists say that bite marks found on a victim's face are a sign that the attacker knew the victim, and, in his rage, the biter was trying to destroy the victim's personality by destroying the face.

# Forensic Odontology and Matching the Marks

Odontologists are dentists. A forensic odontologist deals with dental evidence involved in crimes. The forensic odontologist should study the bite mark before being told about or examining the teeth of any suspects. An "outside-in approach" is used to examine the mark. This means she will look at the biggest features—such as the size of the jaw—first, and the smallest features—like marks left by individual teeth—last.

After examining the bite mark and forming an opinion about the features of the mouth that made it, the odontologist can begin comparing the bite mark to the mouths of suspects, looking for four types of features. The more specific the feature, the fewer possible matches there will be.

Gross features means the largest features of the mouth: the jaws. The forensic odontologist must determine whether a suspect has all the teeth that are seen in the bite mark. He must compare the size of the suspect's arches to the size of the mark, and also compare their shapes to the mark's shape. If these gross features match, then he can move on to compare tooth position.

Several types of tooth position are examined. First, the odontologist makes sure the teeth and the marks are in the same position on the jaws. Then, the direction the teeth are rotated in their sockets are compared to the tooth positions on the marks. The odontologist looks at the position of the teeth relative to each other, as well as their position relative to the bite-line, or where the teeth rest when the mouth is closed. This is called their occlusal position. Finally, the spacing between the teeth is compared.

If these positional features match, the forensic odontologist can look for intradental features, the most individual and exact marks. These are the size

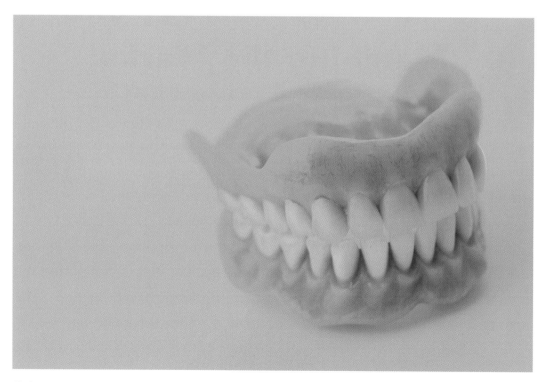

Odontologists examine teeth and bite marks. Like fingerprints, bite marks are unique to individuals and can be used in making identifications.

of the teeth and the ways they are curved, or the exact shape of the teeth. Worn edges are recorded, as are any jagged or broken teeth.

After these features of the actual mouth are examined, the forensic odontologist should look at the suspect's associated features. These are features that could influence the bite and include the state of the tempromandibular joint (TMJ), the joint between the upper and lower jaws. The face's symmetry or asymmetry is examined, as well as the tone and balance of the facial muscles; any scars or signs of surgery must also be noted. The odontologist will measure how far the mouth can open and note any occlusal disharmonies—ways in which the teeth meet when the mouth is closed, such an over- or underbite. He should also record whether the suspect has facial hair and examine whether that could influence the mark. The tongue and the way it contacts the teeth must be examined, and a saliva sample taken for possible DNA comparison.

After these examinations, the forensic odontologist is ready to collect other types of evidence from the suspect. He should locate records of any dental treatment the suspect has had since the date the bite mark was made. He then gathers records of the suspect's teeth and bite pattern.

First the mouth is photographed. The lips are pulled back and the teeth are photographed from the outside, then the mouth is opened and the inner surfaces are photographed. All photographs must be taken with a scale—a ruler held next to the part being photographed to show its size.

An odontogram is prepared, which is a detailed dental chart and record of each tooth. This is done on a card similar to a fingerprint card, only with written information rather than inked prints. Each of the thirty-two human tooth positions is assigned a number, with "#1" indicating the upper-right third molar, and "#32" the lower-right third molar. Each of these numbers is subdivided into the five visible surfaces of the tooth—the front and back, each side, and the top surface. Notes are made on the odontogram describing each tooth and each surface, whether it is missing, worn, repaired, rotated in the socket, or broken.

Two or more impressions of each arch are made, and casts of the teeth are formed with dental stone. Sample bites are produced, usually in dental wax. Casts can also be made of these impressions.

# Bite Marks on Victims and Other Evidence

Collecting and interpreting bite-mark evidence on victims can be much trickier than when the marks are on other types of evidence. When a bite mark is on a victim, the mark was made on a highly variable, soft, moving target. The victim's movements, both in the struggle with the attacker and the movements of the individual cells and tissues in the body's reaction to a wound, greatly influence the marks. Like fingerprints, bite marks can be complete, partial, clear, indistinct, or latent. Also like fingerprints, it is rare to have a clear, complete mark.

When the bite mark is on a victim, the investigator must be able to recognize what a bite mark looks like and take note of the different types of injuries. One bite mark can contain several injuries: abrasions (scrapes); contusions (bruises); lacerations (tears); ecchymosis (small area of bleeding beneath skin); petechiae (burst capillaries); avulsion (tearing of muscles, ligaments, or tendons, sometimes with small bone fractures); indentations (toothmarks); erythema (redness); patterns of materials, such as clothing, that were between the teeth and the flesh.

Like latent fingerprints, latent injuries cannot be seen with the naked eye under normal light. This may be because the surface of the skin is not visibly damaged, including if a wound on a living victim has healed. With

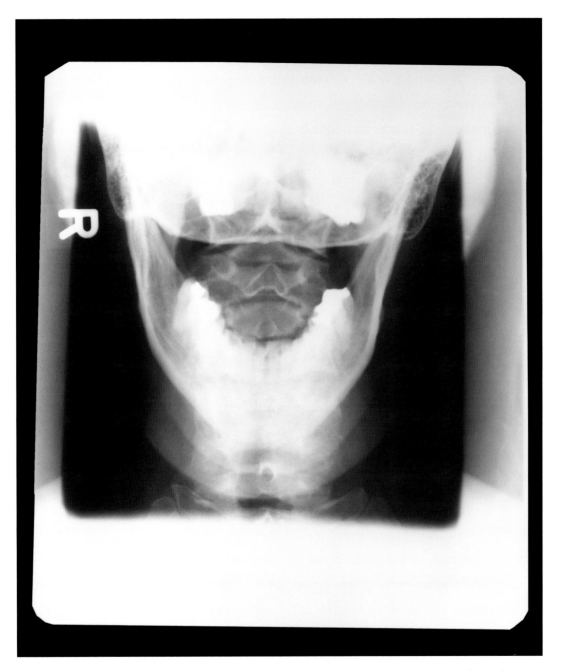

Dental records can be used to compare bite patterns. They can also play an important role in giving names to the unidentified bodies of crime and accident victims.

latent injuries, an ALS is used. This type of light allows investigators to see a wound up to a year after it has healed.

While collecting evidence from the victim and comparing this evidence to the suspect, the investigator must take many factors into account. These things make bite marks on living flesh more difficult to study than bite marks on inanimate objects. The investigator looks at the bite mark's location on the body, and the details and shape of the body part. Is the surface flat, curved, or irregular? What are the tissues' characteristics? What type of tissues are they? Bone, cartilage, muscle, and fat beneath the skin's surface can all affect how the bite mark looks.

Environmental circumstances after the wound was made can also affect its appearance. These include washing or contamination of the wound, change of the victim's position or movement of the body, and on deceased victims, lividity (pooling of blood in areas of the body that are closest to the ground), embalming, or decomposition.

When studying the size of the mark, the investigator must consider whether the skin in the area is able to move, how much the victim was struggling, how deep the bite is, and how the mark is affected by tissue inflammation.

Several types of evidence are collected from victims. Photographs of the wounds are taken. These must be taken with a linear scale, a ruler used to indicate the size of the wound, as well as with a circular scale, which helps show if the camera has caused any distortion of the wound's shape in the photographs. On a living victim, it is best to take a number of photographs over time. ALSs can also be used to look for latent wounds to photograph.

If the wound hasn't been washed and it won't damage the shape of the wound, saliva samples are taken with cotton swabs. If the marks are deep enough, impressions can be made of the wound. On a deceased victim, when it will not destroy evidence, tissue samples are taken, and if possible,

# Tissue Inflammation

As soon as an injury happens to the body, the body's immune system responds. Injury to cells sends chemical messages to nearby blood vessels. These messages make the blood vessels dilate, causing the area to redden and swell. This dilation makes clotting factors, such as the special blood cells called platelets, rush to the wound site to stop any bleeding. White blood cells that fight disease also rush to the site. Meanwhile, hormones such as histamine (involved with immunity) and epinephrine (also called adrenaline—involved with the "fright, flight, fight" response) are flooding the body and affecting all of its systems. These defense systems cause any wound made on a living body to swell and change shape almost immediately. Forensic investigators must understand these changes and take them into account when interpreting marks.

the area of the site is stabilized and collected (removed from the body), then preserved and fixed (placed in an embalming fluid such as formalin).

Dental impressions and oral photographs should also be taken of the victim. These are done for two reasons. First, if the bitten area is a place the victim could have reached with her own mouth, they are taken for comparison. Also, if the victim could have bitten the attacker in self-defense, it is important to know what her bite marks look like to match them to any bite marks found on a suspect.

When bite marks are on evidence besides a body, like food or gum, the entire item is entered as evidence. The bite marks should also be photographed and impressions can be made. The suspect makes test-bites in the same types of substance for comparison.

# Introducing Bite-Mark Evidence in Court

Bite-mark evidence has been admissible in the United States since 1954. Its accuracy, however, is still debated. This is because, even if all human

Forensic scientists don't limit their investigation of bite marks to wounds found on victims. Chewed gum found at a crime scene may help identify a suspect.

bite patterns are unique, the one-of-a-kind features are difficult to see because of the nature of bite marks in tissue. This is why any match is expert testimony, not scientific proof, because it is based on the experience and opinion of the expert making the match.

Since bite-mark matches are difficult to make and even more difficult to prove, forensic odontologists have professional associations that board-certify forensic odontologists and determine guidelines for giving testimony. These guidelines try to define the terminology odontologists use and explain how sure a jury can be that a "match" came from the defendant. It is important to know what these terms mean and how accurate they are to understand what expert testimony is actually saying.

In official forensic odontological terminology, a "point" is any feature that could have been made by a tooth and can be compared to a tooth. A "concordant point" is a feature that corresponds to the mark and to the subject (for example, the mark shows a left canine tooth in the lower jaw, and the suspect has a left canine tooth in his lower jaw). An "area of comparison" is a region, pattern, or area containing multiple points of comparison (all the marks from the teeth of the lower jaw, for example, would make up one area of comparison).

The word "match" alone is not specific; it means any similarity between the mark and the suspect's teeth. When a match is called "consistent" or "compatible," it means there are some similarities. A "possible biter" means the suspect has teeth that are like the perpetrator's, but other people could also have the same sort of teeth; so far, however, there are no inconsistencies between the mark and the suspect's teeth that would rule out the suspect. A "probable biter" means the suspect could have left the mark, and most other people could not have: there are several points that match, some individual identifying characteristics, and no inconsistent evidence.

## Comparison Technology of Trials Past

Before computer technology, tooth marks were hand-traced on a picture of the bite wound and compared with tracings of the teeth made on clear acetate ("transparencies"), or from a photocopy of the dental casts, placed over the bite mark picture. Another technique was to fill the indentations on the suspect's dental casts with metal powder, then photograph the pattern with an X-ray machine. The X-ray was then compared with the bite mark photo.

"Reasonable medical certainty" is considered the highest order of certainty. In this case, the bite mark identifies the suspect as the perpetrator: there are enough individual characteristics to identify this one person and to rule out others, with no inconsistencies. This type of match is considered by the expert to be beyond a reasonable doubt.

In making these matches, the forensic odontologist must compare known to questioned evidence. Known evidence is evidence whose source is known for certain; for example, the odontologist knows that the casts she made of the suspect's teeth came from the suspect. Questioned evidence is the evidence that investigators are trying to identify and match; for example, the bite mark is questioned evidence, and the question is, "Did this mark come from the suspect?"

The most accurate way to compare known to questioned dental evidence is considered to be computerized photo overlays. This means that a digital photo is transposed over a picture of the bite mark to look for points of comparison.

Digital and computer technology has done a lot for the field of forensics. It makes comparisons quicker and more accurate. Today this technology is not only used with fingerprints and bite marks; it is also used for yet another type of print—that left by a human ear.

# Ear Prints: Forensic Markers?

## CHAPTER 5

Some investigators have high hopes that ear printing will someday be as widespread as fingerprinting in criminal investigations. However, these prints remain highly controversial as a form of evidence. Investigators in the United Kingdom, the Netherlands, and Switzerland have worked to create the world's first computerized identification system based on ear prints.

These researchers believe that ear prints are as unique to an individual as fingerprints. They have created a way to take the prints by rolling a thin, plastic material over the ear from bottom to top and lifting the print, as well as lifting latent prints from surfaces using the same techniques that are used for finger-prints.

The most extensive studies on ear prints have been done at the National Training Center for Scientific Support for Crime Investigation in the United Kingdom. However, these studies are said to be research into the uniqueness of the cartilage formation of human ears, not into their usefulness in forensic investigations. The prints, even in these countries, have not yet been widely accepted as evidence. Many countries, such as Australia, do not allow ear prints to be introduced as evidence in courts at all.

# Testing Ear Prints in Court

In North America, the jury is still out, so to speak. Only one famous trial has tested ear-print evidence in the United States at the time of this writing, the 1997 David Wayne Kunze trial, in Washington State. The defendant was accused of bludgeoning his ex-wife's fiancé to death, and of attacking and severely wounding the decedent's thirteen-year-old son. There was little evidence to link Kunze to the crime, and he did not match the description

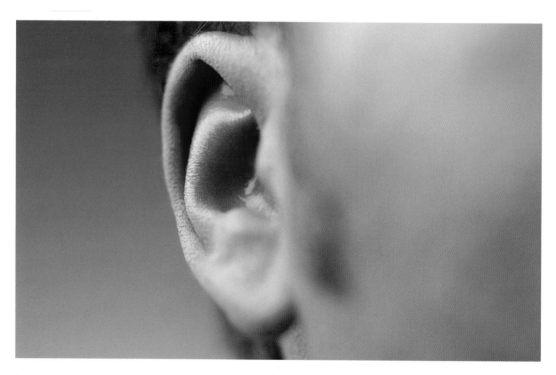

Most courts have ruled that ear prints are not admissible as evidence in trials. This may change as more studies on the ear are conducted.

given by the boy. But while dusting for fingerprints, a technician came across a latent ear print. The technician developed and lifted this print.

When the case went to trial, ear-print researchers from all over the world came to testify. Prints were taken of the defendant's outer ears by coating them with lotion and using different levels of pressure to make prints of them on a glass panel. Researchers hoped they could create a print with the same level of pressure used to make the one left at the crime scene.

Based on these prints, and the testimony of a researcher who insisted that they were "a 100 percent" match, Kunze was convicted and sentenced to life without parole. The story was not over, however.

Kunze continued to declare his innocence, and his attorney continued to claim that ear-printing technology was not scientific. A second trial was granted. This time, the judge discovered that ear-print evidence had not yet been scientifically tested to determine its reliability; it is not even known for sure if all ear prints really are unique, and the FBI does not use this type of testimony as evidence. Based on this unreliability, and the lack of other evidence against Kunze, a mistrial was declared and all charges were dropped, after the defendant had already spent several years in prison.

Supporters of ear printing say that each person's ear cartilage is unique, but skeptics question if this is true. One of the problems with using ear prints as individual identifying characteristics is that the cartilage is malleable. Because the ear is three-dimensional, it can be squished into different shapes, so prints may be neither accurate nor unique, and may be impossible to accurately match. Another problem is that, unlike fingerprints, ears have no ridges—the details that make fingerprints so unique and identifiable. A third problem is that matching these marks can rely heavily on personal opinion rather than objective, computerized data.

Is each ear unique? Perhaps so, but that is much harder for the scientific community to prove because the ear has few points of reference for comparison.

**FINGERPRINTS, BITE MARKS, EAR PRINTS**

Forensic sciences analyze objects or people to establish their unique characteristics, the elements that can lead to the identification of a suspect.

# Forensics:
# A Different Kind of Science

The scientific method has three parts: hypothesis, testing, and theory (or disproval, and going back to the beginning). This means that to test something scientifically, the scientist first makes an educated guess about how something works based on the evidence she has observed. She then tests the hypothesis by making an action happen over and over again under a variety of different conditions. If the hypothesis remains true under all of these conditions, then the scientist forms a theory, which means that all the evidence supports that the hypothesis is a fact.

Forensic science, however, works a bit differently. As one forensics expert puts it, this is because of "a fundamental distinction between forensic science and all other sciences. While science attempts to find unifying themes, forensics attempts the opposite, which is to identify unique objects or people." In other words, most sciences try to find laws that govern how the world works, that are the same all the time and under every circumstance. Forensic science, on the other hand, tries to find what makes each thing in the world different from all others. While experiments can be done that show how processes are the same all the time, it is much harder to prove that something is unique. (Imagine how hard it would be to line up every person in the world, take prints of their ears, and then compare each one to every other one!)

Instead of using the scientific method, forensics uses the *forensic method*: analysis, comparison, evaluation, and verification (sometimes called ACE-V). This means that hypotheses and evidence are examined on a much smaller scale, often with less experimentation. It also means that comparisons, as well as determining when something is a match, are based mostly on the experience of the examiner.

While this can be unreliable, investigators work hard to ensure it is not and that all evidence they present is accurate. Most investigators are highly trained professionals, and most laboratories require that their work be double-checked by others and that investigators take proficiency tests. However, mistakes can still happen because of low-quality evidence, carelessness, inexperience, or because an investigator is biased against a particular suspect and overly eager for his conviction.

In addition to this, caution has to be used whenever a technique is not scientifically proven to be valid, especially in forensic science where people's lives and freedom are at stake. Courts in the United States use two

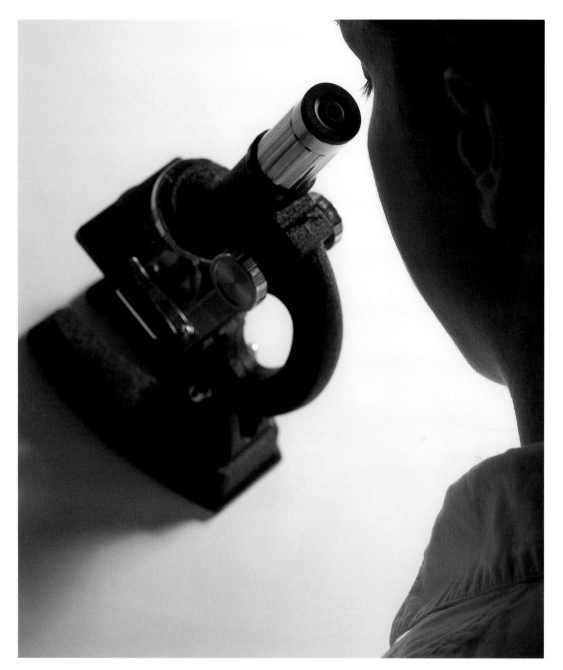

More research must be done on the characteristics of ear prints. Scientists must prove that each ear is unique before courts will allow their prints to be used in trials.

Ear Prints: Forensic Markers?       **75**

A judge carefully weighs arguments for and against the inclusion of scientific evidence at trial. She will also consider Supreme Court rulings in making her decision.

standards to determine if evidence is scientifically accurate: the Frye standard and the Daubert criteria. Both are based on criminal trials.

# Scientific Standards in the Courtroom

The Frye standard comes from a 1923 case called *Frye v. United States*, in which the court decided that in order for forensic evidence to be used, that type of evidence must have "gained general acceptance in the particular field in which it belongs." The Daubert criteria comes from a 1993 case called *Daubert v. Merrill Dow Pharmaceuticals*, where a drug was accused of causing birth defects. The prosecution was not allowed to use evidence from new scientific studies because the type of study had not yet gained general acceptance. The Supreme Court decided that judges are responsible for determining the acceptance and reliability of a scientific technique. The Court also determined that forensic science must have the same standards as other sciences: be testable, subject to **peer review**, and have a known potential rate of failure.

Despite the Court's decision, forensic evidence is not always forced to meet the Daubert criteria. This is because some techniques are considered to have "proven reliability"—meaning they have been used over and over again for a very long time and are considered accurate (such as fingerprinting), and so testing their reliability scientifically is considered unnecessary.

Only time will tell if these criteria will eventually support the use of ear prints as legal evidence. In the meantime, however, forensic investigators and courts make use of these criteria to justify the use of other personal and forensic markers.

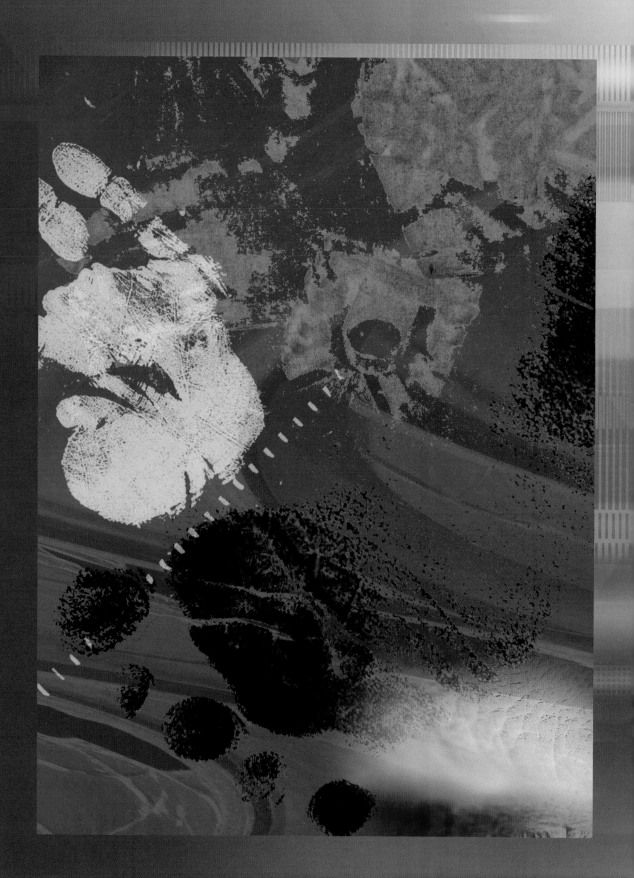

# 6

# Additional Personal and Forensic Markers

As technology improves, more and more ways of identifying people and objects involved in crime scenes are being investigated. The huge success of fingerprints as unique identifying markers has sparked interest in other possible human signposts. Most of these have yet to be tested scientifically and are very new to criminal trials.

## Fingernail Marks

With the individuality of fingerprints and bite marks, some forensic investigators are questioning whether fingernails can leave individual identifying evidence as well. While some people hold out high hopes, so far fingernail marks remain

# Case Study:
# The TellTale Hand

Sometimes the absence of a mark can be as damaging as the mark itself. Authorities in the United Kingdom were confused by the lack of fingernail marks in the 1943 robbery and strangulation of a pub keeper . . . until they arrested a suspect who was missing the tops of his fingers. The defense attorney insisted, based on asking the man to squeeze his hand as hard as he could, that the defendant could not have strangled the victim because his hands were too weak. Though found not guilty, the defendant continued with a life of crime, including breaking and entering. Before his death, he walked into a newspaper office and asked them to publish his written confession of the pub keeper's murder. Newspaper workers noted that despite his truncated hands, his penmanship was perfect.

a class characteristic. These marks are usually used in strangulation cases, where fingernail marks are left around the neck, and in defensive injuries, when marks that the victim left in self-defense may help identify a perpetrator. Scrapings from underneath the fingernails are also helpful in collecting evidence such as fiber, tissues, or DNA, but using fingernail marks to identify individuals with certainty is probably not in the future of forensic science.

# Palm Prints and Handprints

Sometimes palm prints can be used to identify victims and perpetrators. It is estimated that 30 percent of prints found at the scenes of crimes are palm prints. In 2003, the New York and Los Angeles police departments, along with departments in several other large U.S. cities, began to collect palm prints as well as fingerprints with laser scanners and to build computerized palm print databases. Palm prints are also taken from deceased victims.

Occasionally, a palm print may be the only print found at the scene of a crime. This was the case in the 1993 kidnapping of a teenager in Peta-

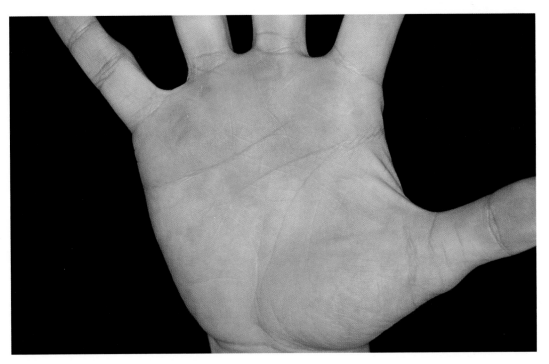

Like fingerprints, palm prints are unique to each individual. Criminals often forget and rest a hand somewhere at the crime scene, such as on a wall while leaning over a victim.

luma, California, who was abducted during a slumber party in her home. Her two frightened friends, who had been tied up by the kidnapper, gave descriptions to the police, but the only evidence was a partial palm print found on a bunk bed railing. Several weeks later, the girl's torn clothes were discovered near a ditch. A car belonging to Richard Allen Davis, on parole for two kidnapping convictions, was found in this ditch. A fingerprint expert matched his palm print to the one on the bunk bed. Davis confessed to the kidnapping and murder, and led police to the girl's body.

Other parts of the hands can leave prints as well. Handprints played an important role in the 1993 murder trial of a police officer in Hawaii ac-

A hand's physical characteristic as seen in a handprint, such as a misshapen finger, can also help identify suspects.

The scientific community has not determined if each person's lips are unique. Because of that, lip prints are not generally used as an identification tool.

cused of killing his wife. The officer first insisted he had accidentally run over his wife while searching for her in a rainstorm; then he said she had been killed in a hit-and-run car accident. The inside of the van where the wife's body was found looked clean; however, when investigators applied the chemical ortho-tolidine, they saw many areas where blood had once been smeared. These areas included blood spatters, marks where the victim's blood-soaked hair had been dragged against the ceiling and walls, and many handprints. The direction of the handprints showed a partially closed fist making a downward motion. These handprints helped investigators discover the true story: the officer had beaten his wife to death with a heavy object inside the van.

# Footprints

Footprints seem to be as individual as fingerprints. Like fingerprints, they have ridges that create loop and whorl patterns and release sweat and skin oils. In fact, the FBI keeps a footprint file of arrested persons who have no fingers. The area behind the big toe is used to classify these prints. There are about four hundred sets of prints in this file.

Like fingerprints, footprints can be plastic, patent, or latent. Latent footprints are developed and recorded in the same way as palm prints and fingerprints. Patent prints can be photographed and saved, and plastic prints can be cast.

One type of footprint study is called forensic barefoot morphology. This is the study of prints left by the weight-bearing areas of the bottom of the foot, rather than by the skin ridges. It can help link a victim or suspect to shoes found at a crime scene (by the impressions left inside of shoes by the feet), or to footprints in mud, blood, or other substances.

Forensic barefoot morphology, especially matching feet to the insides of shoes, has been used in Canadian courts since 1948. Feet are compared to the impressions by making ink prints and by taking photographs, with a scale, of each side of the foot. The impressions inside shoes are saved by cutting the shoe apart, and photographing and preserving the imprints.

# Lip Prints

Lip prints are another type of imprint that some forensic investigators are examining to determine its value in a courtroom. While lip-print evidence has been used in at least one North American murder case, its legitimacy is highly questioned. The FBI does not accept lip-print evidence as individual identifying evidence, and very few scientific studies have been done to test whether lip prints are individual and unique.

# Shoe Prints

Shoe prints can be class evidence, since many different pairs of shoes in the world have the same pattern. However, shoes become individual identifying evidence after belonging to a person. With time, a pair of shoes acquires wear patterns and bits of debris in the soles. The new patterns that are created make each shoe unique. Shoes that have the soles stitched to the bodies also have individual identifying characteristics because stitching is done randomly and is not the same on all shoes.

When a criminal leaves her shoe prints in dust, soil, blood, or any other substance at the scene of a crime, she has left her signature for investiga-

Footprints left by naked feet on surfaces and impressed into soil, sand, and other substances can be used for identification. Science has shown they are as unique as fingerprints.

tors to find. The FBI keeps a record of shoe print patterns from shoe manufacturers. This helps investigators determine the brand of shoe. Once this is known, suspect shoes can be narrowed down, and, once found, the shoe can be matched to the prints by its individual characteristics.

Shoe prints can be latent or visible. Latent prints can be dusted, photographed, and lifted. When the print is plastic, like in snow or mud, it can be cast by spraying the original print with a lubricating sealant, such as acrylic lacquer or shellac, and then making a cast with alginate, plaster, or a special casting wax.

# Tire Tread

Tire-tread prints are unique for the same reason that shoe prints are—the gathering of debris and wear on the tires. They can be cast using the same methods as are used for shoe prints. Once tire prints are collected, they can be matched to a tire manufacturer, which may help investigators narrow their search down to a single vehicle.

Both tires and shoes have an added benefit for investigators: they collect substances with which they come in contact. The tread of tires and shoes may pick up bits of blood, hair, dust, or other substances that can help investigators place a suspect at the scene of a crime.

# Clothing and Other Fabric Prints

Gloves can sometimes leave prints that can be as helpful as actual fingerprints. They can be important because as gloves wear, they become contaminated with debris that makes prints, like oils and sweat, as well as

# Case Study:
# Following the Tracks to a Crime

Many times evidence of a minor crime leads authorities to a much greater one, as Death Valley National Park rangers discovered one September day in 1969. The rangers saw a vandalized bulldozer and followed tire tracks to a stolen vehicle that had crashed into a tree. A neighbor told them about a group of people living on a nearby abandoned movie ranch. The ranch was raided for auto theft, and several people were arrested. While in jail, one of these people confessed to the Los Angeles murder of actress Sharon Tate and five of her friends and houseguests earlier in the year—and as a result, the Manson Family was busted. They were brought to trial for the serial murders of eight people, and five of the "family" members, including Charles Manson and the confessee, Susan Atkins, were sentenced to life in prison.

marks that make the prints original. Each piece of dirt, each tear or crease, makes the glove's print unique. Glove prints can be collected in the same way as fingerprints, only more carefully, since the prints are usually lighter and more delicate. Once investigators have discovered a suspicious glove, they can make comparison prints.

Clothing also contains patterns that can leave prints. This was an important point in an American case in which a husband was accused of

# Case Study:
# Whip Marks Lead to Conviction

One of the most famous cases that was partially solved by imprint marks is the case of serial killer Neville George Clevely Heath. Near the end of World War II, this young man liked to pose as a military officer. After committing the brutal sexual murders of a few young women, his conviction was sealed when a riding whip he carried with him in a briefcase was matched to marks left on the bodies. He was also implicated by bite marks he had left on his victims.

strangling his wife. At first the exact way in which she died was questioned, until the pattern inside the elastic band of her underwear was compared to three marks around her neck. The prints matched; the underwear had been stretched and wrapped around her neck three times, forming a ligature with which she was strangled, and leaving marks so deep they could clearly be seen on the corpse.

# Imprint Evidence
# in the Courtroom

When examining any forensic evidence, judges and jurors must remember that these are not exact, tested sciences. Determining what is and is not a match is based on the experience and opinion of the investigators. Even fingerprint evidence has been called into question recently in North American courtrooms. Forensics is an inexact science, and life and liberty are at stake whenever it is used. The history of criminal justice contains many cases of false convictions and unfair trials, some of them involving fingerprint, bite mark, and other "scientific" evidence.

# "Beyond a Reasonable Doubt": Famous Twentieth-Century Cases of Evidence Gone Awry

The last chapter of Leo Frank's story began on April 26, 1913, in Atlanta, Georgia, when Mary Phagan, a thirteen-year-old who worked at the pencil factory managed by Frank, was murdered. She was found in the basement near a lavatory, sexually molested and strangled with a rope. Two letters framing the night watchman, Newt Lee (who discovered the body), were located near her body. The letters had been written by someone barely literate and said that the murderer was a "tall sleam negro." Another black man named Jim Conley, who happened to be short and rather plump, was in the basement at the time of the murder, but he insisted he had been drunk and unconscious. He also claimed he did not know how to write, and he escaped suspicion.

That suspicion fell instead on Frank, and he was arrested. At that time, Atlanta, like many parts of the United States and Europe, was filled with **anti-Semitism**, and Frank was one of very few Jews in the city. The story was immediately picked up by newspapers, which published sensational articles and headlines about the vicious Jewish sex-murderer.

Meanwhile, it was discovered that Conley could, in fact, write. He admitted he had written the letters found next to the girl's body, but claimed that Frank had ordered him to write them. Frank's trial continued, and the sordid, racist headlines continued to sell newspapers.

Bite marks had been found on the victim's body, marks so clear that the individual tooth prints could be seen. They did not match Frank's teeth. When this evidence did not help the prosecution, it was thrown out of court. The teeth of the one possible witness, Jim Conley, were never compared to the marks. Frank was sentenced to death. Under protest from his attorneys, this sentence was later reduced to life in prison, but the **commuted** sentence did not help Frank.

On August 16, 1915, a mob broke into the prison where Frank was held, took him 125 miles (201 kilometers) away, beat him, tortured him, castrated him, and finally lynched him in the midst of a crowd of around two hundred people. The perpetrators' identities were known, and there were dozens of witnesses—but no arrests were ever made, and no charges filed. Pictures of the lynching were sold as postcards in Georgia for decades.

In 1982, a man came forward who had been another teenage worker in the pencil factory at the time of the girl's murder. He testified he had witnessed Jim Conley with the girl's body but had stayed silent because Conley threatened to kill him if he ever told anyone what he had seen. The State of Georgia pardoned Leo Frank in 1986, but not because of innocence; he was pardoned because the state had failed to protect him while he was in custody.

This case led to the reemergence of the Knights of the Ku Klux Klan; one group was even called the Knights of Mary Phagan. The Anti-Defamation League (ADL) was also founded in direct response to the Leo Frank/Mary Phagan case. The ADL's purpose is to combat anti-Semitism, racism, and bigotry.

A fictionalized account of Frank's story is told in David Mamet's novel, *The Old Religion*.

# 1954—Sam and Marilyn Sheppard

Sam and Marilyn Sheppard and their young son were an all-American family: a young, attractive couple with a growing family, a seven-year-old child

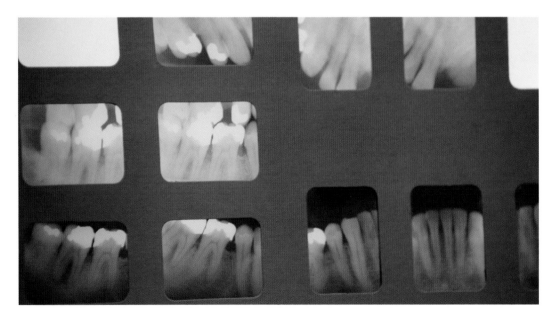

Bite samples may contain specific characteristics already documented in a dental X-ray.

and a new baby on the way, with a home in Cleveland, Ohio, on the shores of Lake Erie. Dr. Sam Sheppard had a successful medical practice—but all that came crashing down on July 4, 1954.

A wounded, distraught, and confused Dr. Sheppard called his best friend early on the morning of July 5, begging him to come to his house immediately, crying that he believed his wife was dead. His best friend also happened to be mayor of the town in which they lived. Soon the house was crowded with not only the friend and his wife, but also Dr. Sheppard's brother (also a doctor), the county *coroner*, and many, many reporters.

As the first to arrive, it is up to the police to maintain the integrity of the crime scene. Otherwise, evidence such as fingerprints can be compromised.

Sam Sheppard spent several years in jail after being falsely convicted of murdering his wife.

Police arrived but did not secure the area or begin gathering evidence. Reporters tramped through the house, including the room where Marilyn Sheppard's corpse lay. She had been severely beaten, her skull smashed, and the bed on which she lay was soaked with blood.

Dr. Sheppard, still dazed and obviously wounded, was taken to a hospital where doctors found his neck had been fractured. According to his story, he had fallen asleep in an armchair after a dinner party he and his wife had hosted. He claimed he awoke to sounds of a struggle, rushed upstairs, and found a man attacking his wife. Dr. Sheppard chased the man out of the house and engaged in a struggle during which he was knocked unconscious. He then spent a period of time on the lakeshore before coming to and returning to the house to find his wife murdered.

While Sheppard was being treated, his home was examined. Parts of the house had been ransacked, and tools and several of the Sheppards' bloodied belongings were found in and near the house. Dr. Sheppard's clothes were examined but no blood was found. The county coroner arrived at the hospital and informed Sheppard, who was sedated and on painkillers, that he believed Sheppard had murdered his own wife.

From the beginning of the investigation, when reporters were allowed free access to the murder scene, important evidence was lost or ignored. A hand-rolled cigarette butt that could have yielded valuable evidence was found floating in a toilet but was flushed by a police officer. Obvious evidence that Marilyn Sheppard had been sexually assaulted was ignored, including the position of her body and her pajamas. The autopsy report made no mention of any signs of rape. A murder weapon was not found. Though the victim's head had been smashed and the entire area soaked with blood, no blood was found on Dr. Sheppard or on his clothing. Finally, a blood trail leading away from the house was never tested.

Like the trial of Leo Frank, the trial of Sam Sheppard drew a great deal of sensational media coverage from the very beginning. Public opinion was heavily against him. Despite the fact that the trial had turned into a media circus and key evidence was lost or ignored, Sam Sheppard was sentenced to life in prison.

After reviewing the circumstances of the trial in 1964, a federal district court granted Dr. Sheppard a new trial. His case went all the way to the U.S. Supreme Court in 1966. This second trial found Sheppard not guilty but couldn't erase the trauma of years in prison convicted of his wife's murder. Sheppard never recovered. The once-successful doctor even tried a stint as a professional wrestler. He died four years later of complications related to alcoholism.

Sam and Marilyn's son tried to clear his father's name by reopening the case in 1996, and made some startling discoveries. The first was that Marilyn Sheppard had been raped—semen not belonging to her husband

Forensic techniques can help investigators determine whether a crime is an example of domestic violence.

was present in her vagina but was never recorded on her autopsy report. Second, two of her teeth had been removed from her mouth as she was beaten to death but not by a blow to the head. They appeared to have been pulled out under great force, meaning that she had probably bitten her attacker. Also, one of her fingernails appeared to have been torn off in the struggle. These theories were consistent with the trail of blood leading away from the house, which blood-pattern experts claim was the type of trail that would have been left by blood dripping from a wound rather than from a murder weapon. Finally, a study of the crime-scene photos revealed that a smear of blood—including a bloody fingerprint—along the closet door next to Marilyn's body had never been tested or used as evidence in the trial.

When criminals such as Richard Eberling, a suspect in the Sheppard murder case, are convicted, a prison like this one is where they often spend the rest of their lives.

In 1988, a man named Richard Eberling was put on trial for the 1983 murder of an elderly woman for whom he was a caretaker. Eberling had apparently killed the woman as part of a plan to collect money from her estate, and was charged with multiple counts of theft and forgery as well. As investigators looked into the case, they discovered Eberling had once been hired to work as a window washer at the Sheppards' home. He was arrested for burglary in 1959, and several pieces of jewelry from the home, including Marilyn's engagement ring, were found on him, yet he was never considered a suspect in her murder.

During the 1997 reinvestigation, DNA from the vaginal swabs, the bloodstains, and the closet were tested. All these proved that a person other than Sam Sheppard had been involved in the crime that night in 1954. The mystery DNA was too degraded for an exact match but was found to be consistent with Eberling's. Eberling also showed a scar consistent with a nail wound on his wrist. During his 1959 arrest, he admitted robbing the Sheppards' home and without being asked about any blood trails by police, said he had accidentally cut himself on a kitchen knife and bled throughout the house. Neither Dr. Sheppard nor Eberling's supervisor as a window washer recalled any blood at the time he was hired. Finally, the bloody fingerprint on the closet door is considered by modern experts to be a match to Eberling's.

Two witnesses came forward, a nurse in 1996 and Eberling's cellmate in 1998, and reported that Eberling had confessed to the rape and murder of Marilyn Sheppard, but he was never tried for this crime. Eberling died in 1998 while in prison on the other murder conviction.

The Sheppard case (which was the inspiration for *The Fugitive*, a popular television show in the 1960s and a movie starring Harrison Ford in 1993) shows the importance of securing the crime scene, gathering evidence properly, and remembering that suspects are innocent until proven guilty.

If investigators had properly handled blood and fingerprint evidence, and if they had looked for bite marks and nail marks on suspects, they might have avoided destroying the innocent lives of Dr. Sheppard and his young son. What's more, they might have put a killer behind bars before he had a chance to kill again.

# 1993—The West Memphis Three

On May 6, 1993, the city of West Memphis, Arkansas, was shocked by the brutal murders of three eight-year-old boys. The boys were found in a ditch, their bodies tied and mutilated.

The hunt for a murderer was over almost before it had begun. Rumors of Satanism abounded in this small, religiously conservative town, and suspicion immediately fell on Damien Echols, a local teenage outcast rumored to practice "witchcraft" and devil-worship. Investigators soon detained Jessie Misskelley, a teenage boy with mental handicaps, and taped a ninety-minute confession obtained during his twelve-hour interrogation.

In this confession, Misskelley claimed to have witnessed and even helped Echols and a friend, Jason Baldwin, murder the boys as part of a Satanic ritual. Despite the fact that Misskelley's report of the crime did not fit evidence found at the scene, his mental handicap, the fact that he was a minor without a parent, guardian, or attorney present, and the fact that he denied the confession later that night, his confession became the basis of the prosecution's case.

Echols, a young man who had past problems with depression, suicide attempts, and running away from home, was convicted in the minds of local residents from the beginning. His interest in Eastern religions and pagan religions such as Wicca cast him as a "devil-worshipper" in the minds of many. The offer of a reward for information incriminating Nichols also brought forth a great deal of sensational testimony, none of which could be proven. The three teenagers were convicted of murder, and Echols was placed on Arkansas' death row. They served out their prison sentences until 2011, when all three were released on a plea deal after new DNA evidence was tested.

This case remains one of the most hotly contested convictions in North America, and some still believe the boys were guilty. Some of the strongest

Wooded areas are popular dump sites for the bodies of murder victims. Many murderers mistakenly believe any evidence will be lost among the leaves and trees.

evidence against the guilty verdict is impression evidence. Shoeprints were found in the area of the bodies that did not match footwear belonging to any of the boys, and an abrasion thought to be from footwear was found on the body of one of the victims. Another victim's body bore the impression of a knife handle, which was never compared to two knives possibly involved in the murder.

The most crucial impression evidence, however, are bite marks. Two of the boys sustained multiple bites, one on his face, the other on his inner thighs. From the beginning of the investigation, these marks were not recorded or investigated properly.

Whenever bite marks are found on a victim, a forensic odontologist should examine them. In this case, however, the bodies were not even examined by a board-certified medical examiner, and autopsies (required in homicide cases) were not performed before the bodies were buried. The bite marks were not entered as evidence at the time of Echols' trial. Instead, they were said by the prosecution to be marks from a serrated knife. During later questioning, it was discovered that the judge trying the case did not know what odontology is.

Due to lack of funds for the defense, many areas of forensic investigation were not pursued during Echols' trial. During the trials of the other two boys, the defense attorney was able to secure the aid of a board-certified forensic odontologist. The odontologist confirmed that the marks were bite marks made by an adult human. He took impressions of the teeth of all three defendants and compared them to the wounds on the victims. None of them matched. In addition, criminal profilers claimed that the bite marks, as well as other wounds and mutilations, were of a type most often found in battered-child homicides, where the victims and the attackers know each other intimately. Evidence of prior sexual abuse was found on two of the

The services of a forensic odontologist may be outside the financial reach of some defendants. But they can be an important tool, as seen in the case of Damien Echols.

"Beyond a Reasonable Doubt"

victims, the two who were most severely sexually mutilated, again pointing to an attacker, or attackers, who knew the victims.

No matter how noble the intent, any system is only as good as the people involved in it. Justice demands expertise, impartiality, and the careful, clear, unbiased thought of judges, experts, law enforcement officers, attorneys, and juries. Just as important, forensic science, no matter how sophisticated and accurate, is worth nothing if it isn't used. We have the technology to bring more accurate evidence before courts now than we have ever had at any other period in history. But it's only good if we use it. Too often, lack of money, lack of interest, bias, and sensationalism prevent the use of every avenue in the quest for justice.

Despite the human shortcomings that limit forensic science, however, it continues to provide us with new and better ways to solve crimes. It gives hope for justice being done and crimes solved. Until the day that human beings stop committing crimes against each other, we can continue to work to solve them as accurately and as fairly as possible, using science as our ally.

# Glossary

**absolve**: To state publicly or officially that somebody is not guilty and not to be held responsible for something.

**anti-Semitism**: Policies, views, or actions that harm or discriminate against Jewish people.

**ballistics**: The study of the movements and forces involved in the propulsion of objects through the air.

**civil rights**: Rights that all citizens of a society are supposed to have.

**commuted**: Reduced a legal sentence to a less severe one.

**coroner**: A public officer whose principal duty is to inquire into the cause of any death in which there is reason to suppose it is not due to natural causes.

**enclosure**: A period in European history when the common areas used for grazing herds of farm animals were fenced in for personal use by the nobility, driving thousands of peasants off the land and into cities.

**entomology**: The branch of zoology that deals with the study of insects.

**feudal**: Relating to a medieval legal and social system in which vassals (servants or tenants) held land from lords in exchange for military service.

**fluoresce:** To emit electromagnetic radiation, especially light, when exposed to radiation or bombarding particles.

**Industrial Revolution**: The social and economic changes in the United States, Great Britain, and Europe in the late eighteenth century that led to the widespread adoption of industrial methods of production.

**labor unions**: Organized groups of workers who fight for their rights, including improved pay and working conditions.

**ligature**: Something used for binding or tying things up.

**papillary lines**: Ridges in the skin covering the palms of the hands and the soles of the feet.

**peer review**: Assessment of an article, piece of work, or research by people who are experts on the subject.

**physiology**: The branch of biology that deals with the internal workings of living things.

**preponderances of evidence**: The superiority in numbers or importance of evidence.

**radial**: Curving toward the radius bone in the lower arm.

**sadists**: People who get sexual pleasure by causing someone else physical or mental pain.

**serfdom**: An economic and social system characterized by serfs, agricultural workers who cultivated land belonging to a landowner and who were bought and sold with the land.

**serology**: The branch of medicine that deals with the study of blood serum and its parts.

**ulnar**: Curving toward the ulna bone in the lower arm.

**Wicca**: A religion based on ancient European pagan religions that worships a goddess, nature, and the earth; practitioners sometimes call themselves "witches."

# Further Reading

Beavan, Colin. *Fingerprints: The Origins of Crime Detection and the Murder Case That Launched Forensic Science*. New York: Hyperion, 2001.

Camenson, Blythe. *Opportunities in Forensic Science Careers*. Chicago, Ill.: The McGraw-Hill Companies, 2001.

Federal Bureau of Investigation. *FBI Handbook of Forensic Science*. New York: Skyhorse Publishing, 2008.

Fridell, Ron. *Solving Crimes: Pioneers of Forensic Science*. New York: Grolier Publishing, 2000.

Friedlander, Mark P., Jr., and Terry M. Phillips. *When Objects Talk: Solving a Crime with Science*. Minneapolis, Minn.: Lerner Publications Co., 2001.

Houck, Max M. *Mute Witness: Trace Evidence Analysis*. San Diego, Calif.: Academic Press, 2001.

Lane, Brian. *Crime and Detection*. New York: DK Publishing, 2005.

Lee, Henry C., and Thomas W. O'Neil. *Cracking Cases: The Science of Solving Crimes*. Amherst, N.Y.: Prometheus Books, 2009.

Pentland, Peter, and Pennie Stoyles. *Forensic Science*. Philadelphia, Pa: Chelsea House Publishers, 2002.

Wecht, Cyril, Greg Saitz, and Mark Curriden. *Mortal Evidence: The Forensics Behind Nine Shocking Cases*. Amherst, N.Y.: Prometheus Books, 2007.

# For More Information

"All About Fingerprints and Other Impressions" by Katherine Ramsland
www.crimelibrary.com/criminal_mind/forensics/fingerprints/1.html

"Bite Marks as Evidence to Convict" by Katherine Ramsland
www.crimelibrary.com/criminal_mind/forensics/bitemarks/1.html

Classroom Projects
www.discoveryeducation.com/teachers/free-lesson-plans/the-science-of-forensics.cfm

Disputed Cases, Contested Evidence
www.truthinjustice.org

Fingerprint Forensic Science Resource Directory
www.dmoz.org/Science/Science_in_Society/Forensic_Science/Fingerprints

Forensics Current Affairs
www.views-from-the-forensics.webs.com

Forensic Science Resource Center
www.forensictrak.com

Ear Prints
www.crimeandclues.com/index.php/forensic-science-a-csi/impression-evidence/18-ear-identification

National Legal Aid and Defender Association: E-Library
www.nlada.org/Civil/Civil_Library

Publisher's note:
The websites listed on this page were active at the time of publication. The publisher is not responsible for websites that have changed their addresses or discontinued operation since the date of publication. The publisher will review and update the website list upon each reprint.

# Index

# Picture Credits

Benjamin Stewart: pp. 21, 22, 23, 64, 101

Corbis: pp. 24, 42, 76, 95

Digital Vision: pp. 20, 38, 46

Dover: pp. 11, 12

Earthstation1.com: p. 14

PhotoDisc: pp. 73, 93, 103

Photos.com: pp. 17, 28, 30, 43, 49, 50, 52, 53, 58, 61, 70, 72, 75, 81, 82, 83, 85, 94, 97, 98

To the best knowledge of the publisher, all other images are in the public domain. If any image has been inadvertently uncredited, please notify Vestal Creative Services, Vestal, New York 13850, so that rectification can be made for future printings.

# Biographies

## AUTHOR

William Hunter lives in Houghton, New York, with his wife, Miranda, and two children, Elspeth and Liam. He is a high school biology and chemistry teacher in upstate New York. He is a graduate of the State University of New York at Buffalo, earning a master's degree in biology. His interest in forensic science led him to complete elective coursework in the forensic science training program at the University of New York at Buffalo. The author has also been involved in the development and testing of a series of forensic science educational activities, as well as a comprehensive activity for a national science conference.

## SERIES CONSULTANTS

Carla Miller Noziglia is Senior Forensic Advisor for the U.S. Department of Justice, International Criminal Investigative Training Assistant Program. A Fellow of the American Academy of Forensic Sciences, Ms. Noziglia served as chair of the board of Trustees of the Forensic Science Foundation. Her work has earned her many honors and commendations, including Distinguished Fellow from the American Academy of Forensic Sciences (2003) and the Paul L. Kirk Award from the American Academy of Forensic Sciences Criminalistics Section. Ms. Noziglia's publications include *The Real Crime Lab* (coeditor, 2005), *So You Want to be a Forensic Scientist* (coeditor, 2003), and contributions to *Drug Facilitated Sexual Assault* (2001), *Convicted by Juries, Exonerated by Science: Case Studies in the Use of DNA* (1996), and the *Journal of Police Science* (1989). She is on the editorial board of the *Journal for Forensic Identification*.

Jay Siegel is Director of the Forensic and Investigative Sciences Program at Indiana University-Purdue University, Indianapolis and Chair of the Department of Chemistry and Chemical Biology. He holds a Ph.D. in Analytical Chemistry from George Washington University. He worked for three years at the Virginia Bureau of Forensic Sciences, analyzing drugs, fire residues, and trace evidence. From 1980 to 2004 he was professor of forensic chemistry and director of the forensic science program at Michigan State University in the School of Criminal Justice. Dr. Siegel has testified over 200 times as an expert witness in twelve states, Federal Court and Military Court. He is editor in chief of the *Encyclopedia of Forensic Sciences*, author of *Forensic Science: A Beginner's Guide and Fundamentals of Forensic Science*, and he has more than thirty publications in forensic science journals. Dr. Siegel was awarded the 2005 Paul Kirk Award for lifetime achievement in forensic science. In February 2009, he was named Distinguished Fellow by the American Academy of Forensic Sciences.

| DATE | | | |
|---|---|---|---|
| | | | |
| | | | |
| | | | |
| | | | |
| | | | |
| | | | |
| | | | |
| | | | |
| | | | |
| | | | |
| | | | |
| | | | |